A NOTE TO PARENTS ABOUT BEING MESSY

Being neat, clean, and orderly is not merely a matter of aesthetics. It is a waste of time to look for something that has been misplaced. It is frustrating to be unable to use something that can not be found. Dirty items seldom work as well as they do when they are clean. Therefore, while being messy might seem more convenient at the outset, it is not more convenient over the long haul.

The purpose of this book is to teach children the importance of not being messy. It also teaches children specific ways to be neat, clean, and orderly.

Reading and discussing this book with your child can help him or her avoid or prevent messes that can be displeasing, frustrating, destructive, or dangerous.

People are more likely to avoid making messes in an area that is clean and orderly. Therefore, the most effective thing you can do to help your child overcome messy tendencies is to create or select a clean, well-ordered environment for him or her. You also need to encourage your child to maintain his or her environment on a continual basis so it will not become too overwhelming to deal with.

This book belongs to:

_____

No part of this publication may be reproduced in whole or in part, or stored in
a retrieval system, or transmitted in any form or by any means, electronic, mechanical,
photocopying, recording, or otherwise, without written permission of the publisher.
For information regarding permission, write to: Scholastic Inc.,
Attention: Permissions Department, 557 Broadway, New York, NY 10012.

Published by Scholastic Inc.
90 Old Sherman Turnpike, Danbury, CT 06816.

SCHOLASTIC and associated logos are trademarks and/or
registered trademarks of Scholastic Inc.

ISBN 0-7172-8577-4

First Scholastic Printing, October 2005

A Book About
Being Messy

by **Joy Berry**

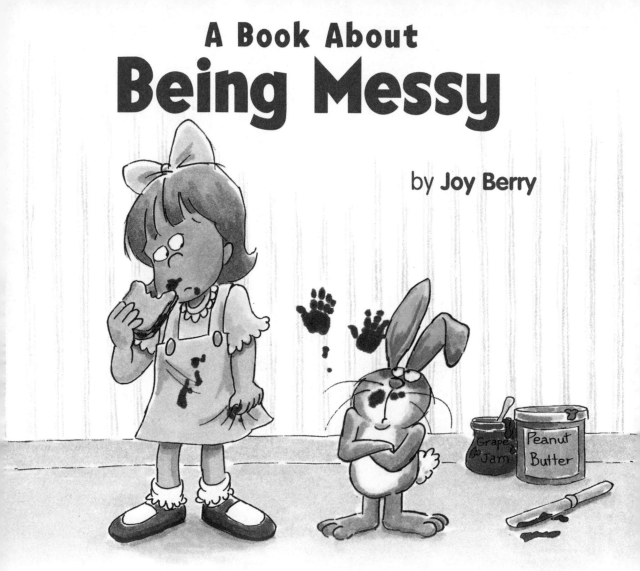

SCHOLASTIC INC.
New York   Toronto   London   Auckland   Sydney
Mexico City   New Delhi   Hong Kong   Buenos Aires

This book is about Annie.

Reading about Annie can help you understand and deal with **being messy**.

You are being messy when you
- spill food on your clothes or
- drop food on the furniture or floor.

You are being messy when you
- walk into clean areas with dirty feet,
- touch furniture or walls with dirty hands, or
- sit on furniture while wearing dirty clothes.

You are being messy when you do not put your trash and garbage in appropriate containers.

You are being messy when you
- do not put things away after you use them,
- do not put things where they belong, or
- do not put things away neatly.

You are being messy when you are careless with things such as crayons, paints, pens, clay, or glue. You are being messy when you get things on your clothes or your surroundings.

A mess can be *displeasing*.

Most people enjoy cleanliness, order, and beauty. A mess is not clean. It is not orderly. It is not beautiful. A mess does not make people happy. It usually makes them unhappy.

A mess can be *frustrating*. People might become upset if they cannot find what they are looking for because
- it is hidden by clutter or
- it is not where it belongs.

A mess can be *destructive*.

- Your clothes and surroundings can be ruined by messy stains.
- Things that are left out can be damaged accidentally.
- Things that are not put away carefully can be ruined.

A mess can be *dangerous*.
- People can slip and possibly fall because of messy spills.
- People can trip over things that are out of place.

Messes can be
- displeasing,
- frustrating,
- destructive, and
- dangerous.

This is why you should not be messy.

An accident can cause a mess. You can avoid accidental messes by *being careful*.

There are things you can do to avoid messes.

To prevent a mess:
- Cover your clothes before you do something that might be messy. (Use a napkin, apron, or smock.)
- Protect the area where you are working by covering it with newspapers, an old sheet, or a tablecloth.

To prevent a mess:

- Keep yourself and your clothes as clean as possible.
- Wash your hands before you touch clean things.
- Get the dirt, mud, or sand off your feet before you walk into a clean area.

To prevent a mess:

- Do not litter. Put trash in a trash container. Put garbage in a garbage disposal or container.
- Put things away when you are finished using them. Put things away neatly where they belong.

You and the people around you will be happier if you avoid being messy.